U0937282

Chinese Cities
Dalian Impressions

中国城市
大连印象

五洲传播出版社
China Intercontinental Press

History
历史
旧梦依稀

Contemporary Times
方今
悠游岁月

History

历史 旧梦依稀

Dalian Museum

A Witness to Modern History

大连博物馆 | 近现代史的见证者

Dalian stands as a witness to the tumultuous modern history of China. The Dalian Museum, situated to the northwest of Xinghai Square in Dalian, is a comprehensive museum dedicated to collecting, displaying, and researching the historical and cultural heritage of the Dalian region. It chronicles the transformation of Dalian from a small fishing village on the Liaodong Peninsula to a bustling international port city over the course of a century. Within this artistic sanctuary, visitors can intimately acquaint themselves with the vicissitudes of Dalian's history since its opening as a port.

大连是中国波澜壮阔的近现代历史的见证者。大连博物馆位于大连市星海广场西北侧，是一座收藏、展示、研究大连地区历史文化的综合性博物馆，记录了大连由辽东半岛的一个小渔村发展为中国国际港口城市的百年历程。在这座艺术殿堂中，人们可以最近距离地了解大连开埠以来的沧桑历史。

Lvshun Museum

A Century of Vicissitudes

旅顺博物馆 | 博物馆的百年沧桑

The Lvshunkou District in Dalian City is known as the "Half of Modern Chinese History." In 1880, during the Qing Dynasty, the Beiyang Fleet was established, and a naval port was built here. Lvshunkou endured the baptism of fire during the First Sino-Japanese War and the Russo-Japanese War. In 1917, Japan occupied Dalian and constructed this building in an eclectic architectural style on the foundation of the unfinished Russian Officers' Club.

The Lvshun Museum is the oldest museum in Northeast China, and for over a century, this slightly weathered small building has housed tens of thousands of collections, including over 200 national treasures. They have witnessed humiliation, resistance, rebirth, and prosperity, narrating the legendary tales of Lvshun, Dalian, and even the entire modern history of China.

大连市旅顺口区有“半部中国近代史”之称，1880 年，清王朝兴办北洋水师，在这里兴建军港。旅顺口经历了甲午战争和日俄战争炮火的洗礼，1917 年，日本侵占大连，在沙俄未建成的军官俱乐部基础上建成这座东西折衷主义风格的建筑。

旅顺博物馆是东北地区最早的博物馆，百余年来，这座略显斑驳的小楼里珍藏着数万件藏品，200 多件国宝级文物。它们经历了屈辱、抗争、新生与繁荣，写下了旅顺、大连，乃至整个中国近代历史的传奇故事。

Trams on Rails

Traversing the Scenic Route of Time

有轨电车 | 穿越时光的风景线

Since 1909, trams 201 and 202 have been gracefully traversing the streets and alleys of Dalian with melodious "ding-ding" sounds. They commence their journey at the break of dawn, harmonizing with the first rays of sunlight, and conclude as the city drifts into slumber, having gracefully traversed over a century, seemingly tireless. Today, the trams on rails in Dalian have evolved into an indispensable and distinctive feature of the local residents' life journey.

从 1909 年开始，201 路、202 路有轨电车就“叮叮当当”地行驶在大连的大街小巷中，它们随着清晨的第一缕阳光开始歌唱，再随着城市的酣睡回归，已经驶过了百余个年头，似乎永不疲倦。今天，大连有轨电车已经成为大连人生活轨迹中不可或缺的一道独特风景。

焖子

Russian-Style Street

Exuding an Exotic Charm in a Romantic City

俄罗斯风情街 | 浪漫之都的异域风情

In 1898, an unequal treaty was signed between the Tsarist Russia and the Qing government, leading to the leasing of Lvshun (Port Arthur) and Dalian. Subsequently, in 1899, the Russian Empire constructed a port and city on the southern coast of Dalian Bay, naming it Dalniy Port, which is now known as the Russian-themed Street.

The unique architectural styles such as "Gothic," "Tower-like," and "Onion Dome" found on this Russian-Style street bear witness to the historical events of Dalian as a port city. As the spring blossoms, the Russian-Style street welcomes the fragrant scent of freshly baked loaves of bread carried by the wind. The ancient buildings bask in the bright sunlight, vibrant yet tranquil, as if recounting the centuries-old vicissitudes of the past.

1898年，沙皇俄国与清政府签订不平等条约，租借旅顺、大连。1899年，沙俄在大连湾南岸筑港建城，命名为达里尼自由港，其行政区域便是如今的俄罗斯风情街。

"尖式""塔式""洋葱头"……这条俄式风情街道上独特的建筑风格见证了大连这个港口城市的历史往事。春日花开，俄罗斯风情街迎风飘来大列巴的香味儿，古老的建筑沐浴在明艳的阳光下，鲜活而静谧，仿佛讲述着过往的百年沧桑。

Contemporary Times

方今 悠游岁月

Dinosaur Sea Exploration Landscape at Jinshitan

A Marine Erosion Miracle from Millions of Years Ago

金石滩恐龙探海 | 亿万年前的海蚀奇迹

A towering, lifelike rock dinosaur, reaching up to 40 meters in height, extends its massive head into the azure sea; this is the "Dinosaur Sea Exploration" landscape in the Jinshitan National Tourist Resort in Dalian, also known as the "Sea Erosion Arch Bridge." Over millions of years, weathering and sea erosion have sculpted the coastal landscape here, turning Jinshitan into a natural geological museum. Giant elephants drinking, fierce tigers pouncing on prey, majestic eagles spreading their wings... Rocks dating back to the Sinian period 600 million years ago are scattered along the coastline, each displaying unique and vivid.

一只高达 40 米，栩栩如生的岩石恐龙，将巨大的头颅伸入蔚蓝的大海中，这就是大连金石滩国家旅游度假区里的“恐龙探海”，又名“海蚀拱桥”。亿万年的风化及海水侵蚀形成了这里的海蚀地貌，金石滩成为一座天然的地质博物馆。大象吸水、猛虎扑食、大鹏展翅……诞生于 6 亿年前震旦纪的岩石散落在海岸线上，形态各异，栩栩如生。

Dalian Forest Zoo

Returning to the Wild World

大连森林动物园 | 回归野生世界

The golden hues of dawn delicately cascade over the towering trees, as the animals of Dalian Forest Zoo embark on a brand new day. Here, one can find endearing and innocent giant pandas, golden snub-nosed monkeys, and alpacas, as well as majestic and formidable polar bears, tigers, lions, and black bears. Some of them leisurely stroll in semi-open areas, while others nap behind crystal-clear glass enclosures. There are also those who roam the forest in search of their wild prey, creating a scene of perfect harmony.

金色的晨曦轻盈洒过高高的大树，大连森林动物园里的动物们又开启了崭新的一天。这里有可爱懵懂的大熊猫、金丝猴、羊驼，也有威猛强悍的北极熊、老虎、狮子、黑熊，它们有的在半开放区域散步，有的躲在晶莹剔透的玻璃幕墙后打盹儿，也有的在森林中寻觅着自己的野味，一切都是那么融洽、和谐。

Oriental Water City

A Poetic Abode on the Waters

大连海昌东方水城 | 水上诗意栖居

Adjacent to the Donggang Pier, a picturesque scene unfolds where sunlight, pigeons, gondolas, and a Renaissance-style castle harmonize effortlessly on the azure eastern coast, creating the enchanting spectacle of Dalian's Oriental Water City. Within the vast expanse of several hundred thousand square meters, an artificial canal meanders through the neighborhood, linking numerous European-style buildings. As the gondolas glide along the canal, creating ripples that dance in the breeze, passengers may find themselves momentarily transported to another realm.

东港码头旁，阳光、鸽子、贡多拉、文艺复兴式的城堡，在蔚蓝的东方海岸交相辉映，毫无违和感，这就是大连海昌东方水城。在数十万平方米的街区内，人工运河蜿蜒前行，连接着数百座欧式建筑。当驳船推开运河水，任凭水花随风荡漾，船上的人也许会恍惚自己身置何方。

Dalian Laohutan

A Picturesque and Romantic Marine Stage

大连老虎滩 | 唯美浪漫的海洋舞台

Upon stepping into the Laohutan Scenic Area in Dalian, one is immediately captivated by its magnificent views. Nestled between mountains and the sea, this area spans 1.18 million square meters, boasting over 4,000 meters of winding coastline. It serves as a world for marine animals and birds, while also offering stunning coastal scenery.

In the very heart of Laohutan Square, stands an array of uniquely shaped tiger sculptures, the largest granite animal stone carvings in China. Six tiger heads face towards the east, exuding a majestic presence. Along the winding coastline, lie a dozen or so sailboats of various sizes and shapes, each evoking the spirit of the Age of Discovery at a mere glance.

踏入大连老虎滩景区的瞬间，就会被其壮观的景致所折服。这里依山傍海，占地面积 118 万平方米，有着 4000 余米的曲折海岸线，既是海洋动物和鸟类的世界，又有绝美的海滨风光。

在老虎滩广场的正中央，矗立着形态各异的群虎雕塑，这是全国最大的花岗岩动物石雕，六只虎头面朝东方，威风凛凛。曲折的海岸线上，摆放着十几艘大小、形状各异的帆船，只望一眼，耳边就仿佛响起大航海时代的号角。

Dalian Sun Asia Ocean World

A Fantastical Theme Park

大连圣亚海洋世界 | 梦幻主题乐园

In July and August each year, Dalian Sun Asia Ocean World transforms into a magical fairytale castle amidst the laughter of children.

Dalian Sun Asia Ocean World stands as the first submarine tunnel-style aquarium in China, as well as the pioneering immersive marine-themed amusement park. Dancing with beluga whales, and frolicking with jellyfish, the 118-meter underwater tunnel acts as a magical wizard draped in an azure cloak, guiding children towards the profound and boundless ocean. It enables them to explore and embrace the endless possibilities of the future in a mysterious, magnificent, and extravagant world.

每年七八月份的大连圣亚海洋世界，总会在孩子们的欢笑中，幻化成一片梦幻的童话城堡。

大连圣亚海洋世界是国内第一座海底通道式水族馆，也是首座情景式海洋主题乐园。与白鲸共舞，与水母嬉戏，118 米的海底通道如同一位身着蔚蓝色披风的魔法师，引领着孩子们走向深邃无垠的海洋，让孩子们在神秘、瑰丽、夸张的世界，探索和挑战无尽的未来。

Breeze of the Sea

海风 漫步自然

Lvshun Naval Port

A Golden Waterway Witnessing Significant Chapters in Modern History

旅顺军港 | 黄金水道写就半部中国近代史

The Lvshun Naval Port, strategically located at the throat of the Yellow and Bohai Seas in Northeast Asia, stands as a rare ice-free harbor. Constructed in 1890, it quickly became a coveted strategic target for powers such as Japan and Russia. The Lvshun Naval Port is strategically advantageous, being easily defensible yet difficult to attack, resembling a closed bay harbor. Today, a portion of the area has been transformed into the Lvshun Naval Port Park, where visitors can witness the majestic sight of the two mountains facing each other to form the entrance to the sea. The newly developed Lvshun New Port serves as the "golden waterway" between the Liaodong Peninsula and the Shandong Peninsula. If one is fortunate, they may even have the opportunity to witness the impressive sight of naval warships entering and exiting the Lvshun Naval Port.

旅顺军港地处黄渤海咽喉要冲，是东北亚地区难得的不冻良港，1890年建成后不久，就成为日俄等列强争夺的战略目标。旅顺军港在战略上易守难攻，近似一个封闭海湾港，如今，部分区域已开放为旅顺军港公园，游客可以在这里看到两山对峙而成的出海口。新开辟的旅顺新港是辽东半岛和山东半岛之间的“黄金水道”，如果运气绝佳，你还能亲眼看见海军军舰进出旅顺军港的威武场面。

Gang Dong Fifth Street

Witnessing the Grandeur of Large Ships and Capturing Magnificent Scenes

港东五街 | 看大船拍大片

On the Gang Dong Fifth Street hailed as the "most beautiful road to the sea," every morning around 10:50 when a gallant female mounted police officer rides her majestic horse slowly past, a specially designated photo area facing the sea is crowded with hundreds of citizens and tourists holding various devices. Soon, at the end of the street one kilometer away, the anticipated cruise ship slowly appears on the sea, framed by towering buildings on both sides, enhancing the already picturesque seascape and making it even more aesthetically pleasing and vibrant. At the moment when the sound of cameras fills the air, what is left behind is the visually refreshing and ever-changing romance of Dalian.

在"通向大海的最美公路"——港东五街上，每逢上午 10 时 50 分左右，当英姿飒爽的女骑警骑着高头大马缓缓走过时，与大海相对的专门拍照区域都会簇拥着手持各式设备的数百名市民和游客。很快，1 公里外街尽头的海面上，期待中的客轮缓缓现身，两侧高大楼宇的衬托，让本就海天一色的构图，显得更加唯美治愈、活色生香，相机声响起的那一刻，留下的是浪漫大连常新常变的视觉新鲜。

Fisherman's Wharf

A Brightly Lit Eastern Fishing Port

渔人码头 | 灯火通明的东方渔港

The Fisherman's Wharf was established in 1930 as a humble fishing port. It wasn't until the 1990s, during the urban development of Dalian, that the concept of "Fisherman's Wharf" was introduced, leading to the influx of cafes, bars, and boutiques. Situated at the Fisherman's Wharf, facing the Binhai Road to the north and overlooking the Yellow Sea to the south, one can truly sense the harmonious coexistence of mountains and seas. As the sun sets in the west, seagulls soar freely in the sky, while old fishing boats come to a rest. In this moment, the simplicity of a Chinese fishing village blends seamlessly with the warmth of European and American fishing ports, blending at Fisherman's Wharf.

渔人码头始建于1930年，最初只是个普通渔港，直到20世纪90年代，大连城市发展，引进“渔人码头”概念后，咖啡、酒吧、小店纷至沓来。身处渔人码头，北临滨海路，南望黄海，感受山海相依。夕阳西下，漫天的海鸥自由飞翔，老旧的渔船停歇下来，中国渔村的质朴，和欧美渔港的热忱在这一刻是如此融洽。

Bangchui Island

The Immortals' Penglai Island Nestled Against Mountains

棒棰岛 | 依山而居的海上蓬莱

The Bangchui Island is surrounded by mountains on three sides, with one side facing the sea. Located 500 meters away from the shore, it is named after its resemblance to a giant *bangchui* (a wooden stick to beat laundry in washing) entering the sea.

Driving or strolling along the verdant path, one can reach the Bangchui Island beach to indulge in the unique romance of the seaside. The misty mountains, shimmering waters, crystal-clear sea, and soft sands make this a cherished holiday memory for the people of Dalian.

棒棰岛三面环山，一面临海，因离岸 500 米外，宛如巨大的“棒棰”入大海的小岛而得名。

沿着绿草如茵的小径驱车或者漫步，可以到棒棰岛海水浴场享受海边独有的浪漫，山色空蒙、水光潋滟、海水清澈、沙质轻柔，这里是大连人最亲切的假日回忆。

Yinshatan Bathing Beach

The Most Beautiful Sunset in Dalian

银沙滩 | 大连的最美日落

Yinshatan Bathing Beach is located on the eastern section of Binhai Road in the Xigang District of Dalian City. The sunset at Yinshatan Bathing Beach is acclaimed as the most beautiful sight in Dalian. Standing on the winding path in front of Yinshatan Bathing Beach, one can admire the quaint scenery of the observation deck of Lianhua Mountain in the distance, while being greeted by the deep azure sea right before their eyes. As the sky gradually darkens, the horizon is adorned with crimson clouds that seem to be shattered into glistening golden fragments by the sea. The elongated shadow of the cross-sea bridge on the water sways slightly in the dazzling sunset, capturing this unique sense of romance in a hazy moment.

银沙滩，位于大连市西岗区滨海路东段。银沙滩日落，被誉为大连最美的景观。站在银沙滩前蜿蜒的小路上，远处是莲花山观景台的别致风光，眼前是蔚蓝幽深的大海。天空慢慢暗下来，满天的红霞仿佛被海水摇成波光粼粼的金色碎片。被海面拉长了的跨海大桥的影子，在绚烂的夕阳中微微晃动着，把这份独有的浪漫，定格在朦胧的瞬间。

Wandering

漫游 城市记忆

Zhongshan Square

A Blooming Flower in the Heart of the City

中山广场 | 宛若盛开的花朵

The birth of Zhongshan Square laid the foundation for the urban layout of Dalian during the periods of the Russian occupation and Japanese occupation. With the square as the focal point, ten main roads extend radially in all directions, resembling a flower blooming in the city. In 1946, in honor of Mr. Sun Zhongshan (Sun Yat-sen), it was renamed Zhongshan Square, a name that has been retained to this day.

The century-old Zhongshan Square in Dalian possesses a unique urban aesthetic and historical memory. Today, it is still surrounded by numerous buildings in Renaissance, classical, Gothic, and Baroque styles. As night falls, the square lights up with brilliance, cars flow through, and citizens gather on the open-air stage to dance gracefully to the music, earning it the moniker of "Zhongshan Music Square."

中山广场的诞生奠定了沙俄和日占时期大连的城市布局，以广场为中心，十条大路呈放射状延伸至四面八方，宛若一朵盛开在城市里的花朵。1946年，为了纪念孙中山先生，这里名为中山广场，沿用至今。

拥有百年历史的中山广场有着独属大连的城市美学和历史记忆。如今，依然簇拥着诸多有着文艺复兴风格、古典主义建筑风格、哥特式风格、巴洛克风格的老建筑。每逢夜幕降临，这里灯火璀璨，车流穿梭，市民云集在露天舞台上随着乐声翩翩起舞，使它又拥有了“中山音乐广场”的美称。

Xinghai Bay Cross-Sea Bridge

A Magnificent Seascape with Unparalleled Grandeur

星海湾跨海大桥｜气势如虹的海上风景线

Whenever the sun sets in the west, it marks the most exquisite moment at the Xinghai Bay Cross-Sea Bridge. This 6.8-kilometer-long bridge resembles a colossal dragon lying horizontally between the mountains and the seas, standing guard over Dalian.

The Xinghai Bay Cross-Sea Bridge was completed in 2015, marking China's first large-span double-deck cable-stayed bridge constructed over the sea with anchorage blocks. It set a record for the heaviest single-section steel truss beam installation in China. Spanning across the shimmering sea, the Xinghai Bay links the land and the ocean in a harmonious blend of colors, reflecting the golden hues of urban life.

每当夕阳西下，就到了星海湾跨海大桥最美的时刻。这座长 6.8 公里的大桥，如同一条横卧在山海之间的巨龙，守卫着大连。

星海湾跨海大桥建成于 2015 年，是中国首座海上建造锚碇的大跨度双层悬索桥，创造了国内最重单节钢桁架梁吊装纪录。星海湾穿梭于波光粼粼的海面，连接着海天一色的陆地和海洋，还有鎏金般的城市岁月。

Xinghai Square

A New Landmark of Fashionable Dalian

星海广场 | 时尚大连的新地标

The Xinghai Square, nestled against the boundless ocean, is where the people of Dalian come to embrace the wind, tread upon the waves, feed the seagulls, and savor coffee. A gentle breeze caresses their faces as the colors of the sky blend with the beauty of the coastline, leaving onlookers breathless.

The entire square is lush with green grass, and the line of navigational stone pillars and lamps leads directly to the sea. Walking south from the central square, one encounters the "Century-old City Sculpture," culminating in an open book-shaped plaza symbolizing the opening of a new chapter for Dalian a hundred years from now. Running through the square from north to south is the central promenade, adorned with a fountain water feature avenue. As night falls, the square is illuminated by lights resembling sparkling stars, and the dancing water droplets of the fountain move to the rhythm of the music, inviting one to revel in a dreamlike scene.

星海广场背靠无垠大海，大连人在这里迎风踏浪，喂海鸥，喝咖啡，柔和的微风拂过脸颊，天空的色彩与海岸线美得令人屏息。

整个广场绿草茵茵，航标石柱灯一线排开直通大海。从中心广场南行，便是“百年城雕”，尽头是翻开的书形广场，寓意着百年后的大连又翻开了新的一页。贯穿广场南北的中央长廊，建有喷泉水景大道，每逢夜色降临，广场上星光璀璨，喷泉跳跃的水珠伴随音乐的节奏，纵情起舞，场面如梦似幻。

Dalian Binhai Road

Adorned by Fresh Flowers and Vast Seas

大连滨海路 | 左手鲜花右手大海

The Binhai Road is situated along the eastern and southern coast of Dalian city, spanning approximately 40 kilometers. It resembles a string of resplendent pearls, adorning the exquisite coastline with its radiance.

On the left side of the Binhai Road lies a mixed forest of coniferous and broad-leaved trees, where in the bright spring sunshine, vibrant azaleas and clusters of cherry blossoms bloom in competition. On the right side stretches the vast and misty sea. Strolling along the wooden boardwalk, one is greeted by the panoramic view of the blue sky, azure sea, verdant hills, white stones, undulating coastline, and scattered fishing boats...

滨海路位于大连市区东部及南部沿海，全长约40公里，仿佛一串光华润泽的珍珠，挂在绝美的海岸线上。

滨海路左侧是针阔叶混交林，春光明媚时，明快的杜鹃花、簇拥的樱花竞相绽放；右面则是烟波浩渺的大海。在木质栈道上漫步，扑面而来的，是蓝天、碧海、青山、白石，连绵起伏的海岸，星星点点的渔船……

Dalian International Conference Center

A Pearl between the Mountains and the Sea

大连国际会议中心 | 山海间的明珠

Dalian's Donggang Business District is hailed as "the Victoria Harbour of the North." After land reclamation and over a decade of transformation, it is now filled with towering skyscrapers. Here, you can experience the bustling vibrancy of a modern metropolis while also unexpectedly encounter the artistic atmosphere hidden within the concrete and steel. The melodious music fountains, the romantic charm of the Oriental Water City, and the luxurious experience of the international yacht harbor all contribute to the unique allure and character of the Donggang Business District.

In the midsummer of 2024, the highly anticipated Davos Summer Forum was held at the Dalian International Conference Center in the Donggang Business District. Resembling a giant shell floating on the sea, the Dalian International Conference Center is themed around "mountain and sea" and vividly represents Dalian's geographic location with mountains behind and the sea in front. Its interior is also filled with a sense of science fiction, making one feel as if they have stepped into a plaza, road, or overpass within the city of Dalian. Consequently, it is praised as "a city within a building, and a building within a city."

大连东港商务区被誉为北方的维多利亚港，经过填海造地与十余年蜕变，如今已高楼林立。在这里，你可以感受到现代都市的繁华与喧嚣，也能在不经意间邂逅那些隐藏在钢筋水泥中的文艺气息。音乐喷泉的悠扬旋律、东方水城的浪漫风情、国际游艇港的奢华体验，构成了东港商务区独有的魅力与风情。

2024 年仲夏，万众瞩目的达沃斯夏季论坛在东港商务区的大连国际会议中心召开。大连国际会议中心仿佛漂浮在海面上的巨大贝壳，其建筑以“山海”为主题，形象地表现了大连背山面海的地理位置，其内部也充满了科幻感，让人仿佛走进了大连城市里的广场、道路、立交桥……人们称赞它为“城市中的建筑，建筑中的城市”。

图书在版编目（CIP）数据

中国城市 ： 大连印象 ： 汉、英 / 陈曦著. -- 北京 ： 五洲传播出版社， 2024. 9. -- ISBN 978-7-5085-5252-1

Ⅰ. K293.13

中国国家版本馆CIP数据核字第2024K9A340号

中国城市：大连印象
Chinese Cities：Dalian Impressions

出 版 人：关　宏

责任编辑：杨　雪

助理编辑：汪梦琦

插　　画：王建华　玖玥工作室

文　　字：陈　曦

译　　者：潘英赵

设计策划：山谷有魚

装　　帧：张伯阳

出版发行：五洲传播出版社

地　　址：北京市海淀区北三环中路 31 号生产力大楼 B 座 6 层

邮　　编：100088

发行电话：010-82005927，010-82007837

网　　址：http://www.cicc.org.cn，http://www.thatsbooks.com

印　　刷：北京市房山腾龙印刷厂

版　　次：2024 年 9 月第 1 版第 1 次

I S B N：978-7-5085-5252-1

开　　本：889mm × 1194mm　1/32

印　　张：6

字　　数：20 千

定　　价：49.8 元